TREASURY OF LITERATURE

Take-Home Books

VOLUME 2

TO ACCOMPANY
BLUE WATERS
AND HOLD ON TIGHT

HARCOURT BRACE & COMPANY
Orlando   Atlanta   Austin   Boston   San Francisco   Chicago   Dallas   New York
Toronto   London

Copyright © by Harcourt Brace & Company

All rights reserved. No part of this publication may be reproduced or transmitted in any form or by any means, electronic or mechanical, including photocopy, recording, or any information storage and retrieval system, without permission in writing from the publisher.

Permission is hereby granted to reproduce the Copying Masters in this publication in complete pages for instructional use and not for resale by any teacher using TREASURY OF LITERATURE.

Printed in the United States of America

ISBN 0-15-303598-6

1 2 3 4 5 6 7 8 9 10   082   97 96 95 94

CONTENTS

Grade 1/Volume 2/Anthologies 4, 5

BLUE WATERS

Unit 1
What Dee Dee Saw (D.W. All Wet)
A Red Boat (Jenny's Journey)
Kenya's Friends (Sea Frog, City Frog)
Who Are We? (Punky Goes Fishing)
A Real Frog (Father Bear Comes Home)

Unit 2
The Egg Tree (The Cake That Mack Ate)
My Friend, Judy (Lionel at Large)
The Flying Turtle (Frog and Toad Together)
Baby Day (The Doorbell Rang)

HOLD ON TIGHT

Unit 1
Go to Sleep! (Peace at Last)
Marco's Day (Dreams)
Sunny and Funny Bunny (Stars)
Where's the Kitten? (There's an Alligator Under My Bed)

Unit 2
The Flower (Henry and Mudge in Puddle Trouble)
Toot the Tugboat (All About Seeds)
Hap's Surprise (Henny Penny)
A Day at the Park (Lost!)
The Big Cake (Jamaica's Find)

TAKE-HOME BOOK
BLUE WATERS
Use with "D.W. All Wet."

HARCOURT BRACE & COMPANY

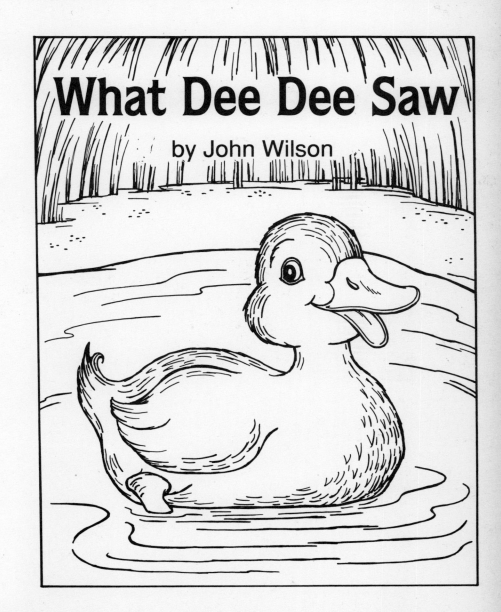

What Dee Dee Saw
by John Wilson

Harcourt Brace & Company material copyrighted under notice appearing earlier in this work.

Now when Dee Dee goes out for a swim, all her duck friends go, too!

Dee Dee was not like her duck friends. They liked to swim just at the beach.

"I like to go way out in the water and swim all over," said Dee Dee. "I'm going to take a swim." And off she went.

Dee Dee saw a big duck out in the water.

"Hello," she quacked. "Would you like to come swimming?"

The big duck did not quack back.

"You see," said Dee Dee. "If you swim way out, you see more!"

"Yes, yes," said her friends. "We will do that. Thank you, Dee Dee!"

"Look!" yelled Dee Dee. "There they are!"

"Dee Dee said so!" her friends said. "The trees are flipped over in the water."

"Don't you like to swim?" asked Dee Dee.

The big duck didn't say.

"This duck is not going to make friends," said Dee Dee.

At last, she went back to the beach.

Dee Dee got out of the water to stand by her friends.

"I just saw a duck that did not quack or swim," said Dee Dee.

"That isn't so!" said her friends.

"But I SAW it," said Dee Dee. "I'm going back out to see more."

Dee Dee took her mother and her father and her friends in the water. Dee Dee's friends saw the duck.

"Look, just like Dee Dee said! This duck cannot quack or swim!" they said.

"Now let's go see the trees flipped over in the water," said Dee Dee.

"I saw a duck that didn't swim or quack. Then I saw a spot with trees flipped over," said Dee Dee.

"Let's all go and see," said Dee Dee's father.

Dee Dee went way out in the water. She saw the duck that did not quack or swim.

"I'll just keep going," she said.

Then Dee Dee came to a spot with lots of trees in the water.

"Why are the trees flipped over in the water?" asked Dee Dee.

Dee Dee looked and looked. At last, she went back to the beach.

"I just saw trees flipped over in the water," said Dee Dee.

"That isn't so!" said her friends.

"Stop saying it isn't so," said Dee Dee's mother. "Now, what did you see, Dee Dee?"

TAKE-HOME BOOK
BLUE WATERS
Use with "Jenny's Journey."

HARCOURT BRACE & COMPANY

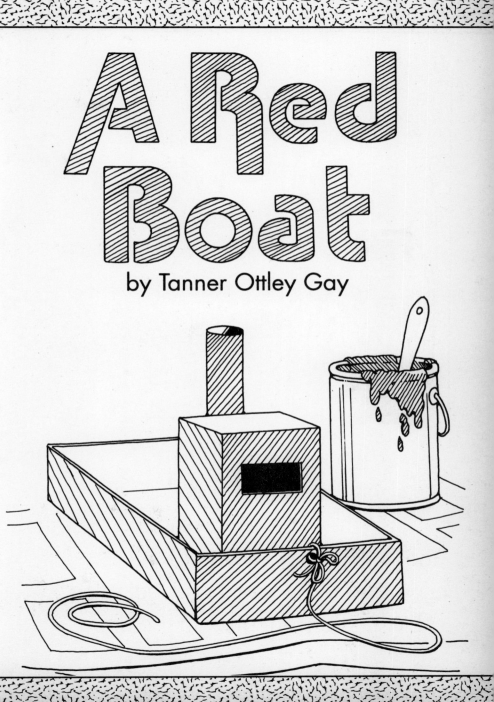

A Red Boat
by Tanner Ottley Gay

Harcourt Brace & Company material copyrighted under notice appearing earlier in this work.

"Look at all the boats!" said Rick.

"There are a lot of boats now," said Jill, "and there will be more!"

"See what I wrote! We can all make boats together."

Rick and Jill went to visit Ben. On the way back, they stopped to look at little boats in the water.

"Look at all the boats!" said Jill.

Rick was standing in the shadow of the trees. He felt sad. He looked as if he was going to cry.

"Why are you sad?" asked Jill.

"Look at all the boats," said Rick. "I want a boat, too!"

"Let's bring this," said Rick.

"Good!" said Jill. "I'll bring this."

Rick and Jill went back to make boats.

"Rick!" said Jill. "Come here! You can make a red boat! We can make boats here."

Rick and Jill went back to the house.

10

"If you would like a boat, we can make one," said Jill.

"But how?" asked Rick.

"I'll tell you when we get back to the house," said Jill. "Come on."

3

"This will be our boat," said Jill.
"How can that be a boat?" said Rick.
"Like this," said Jill.

Just then, Jill and Rick saw two boys standing in the shadow of the trees. "Look at all the boats," one boy said. "I want a boat, too."

Jill and Rick went back with the boat. When they put it in the water, a girl and her friends said, "What a good boat!"

"Thanks!" said Jill and Rick.

"What kind of boat do you want?" asked Jill.

"I want a red boat," said Rick.

"Then you will have a red boat," said Jill.

Jill cut the box open so they could make the boat.

"Now we can go back with our boat," said Rick.

TAKE-HOME BOOK
BLUE WATERS
Use with "Sea Frog, City Frog."

HARCOURT BRACE & COMPANY

Kenya's Friends

by Carol Peske

Harcourt Brace & Company material copyrighted under notice appearing earlier in this work.

Kenya looked at her friends. Each one looked very happy. Kenya put them all in the little house.

"Thank you, friends," said Kenya. "Here is your home."

Kenya and her mother were fixing up a little house together. The house looked very nice.

Then Kenya's dog jumped up and pulled on the side of the house. The house fell down, and the front came off.

"Oh, no!" said Kenya. "Now what will we do?"

"Go to bed now," said Mother. "We will fix it in the morning."

"Then it could only have been my friends," said Kenya as she held Cow.

"Your friends?" asked Dad.

"They are the only ones that could have fixed it," Kenya said.

Kenya's house was for friends like Bird and Cow. She had been wishing they could sleep in the little house that night.

"Dad, did you fix the house?" asked Kenya.

"No, I have been asleep," said Dad.

Every night Kenya would hold each friend and say good night.

"Good night, Bird and Cow," said Kenya. Then she held Frog and Lion. "Good night, Frog and Lion. I wish you could sleep in the little house now. Mother and I will fix your house in the morning."

"Mother! Dad! Come see the house. It's all fixed!"

"Did you fix it?" asked Mother.

"No, did you?" asked Kenya.

"No, I have been in bed," said Mother.

That night, when Kenya was asleep, her friends were awake.

"Kenya is very nice to us!" said Cow. "If only we could tell her how much we like her."

"Yes!" said Lion. "She is fixing up a little house just for us. Why don't we all fix the house for her?" asked Lion.

When Kenya got up, she looked at the house.

"Oh, look!" she yelled. "The house is all fixed!"

She looked at each side of the house. It all looked very nice.

"Yes!" said Frog.

"All right!" said the friends. "Let's do it now!"

It was a bright night, so they could see very well. Each one fixed a little bit of the house.

It took them all night. At last, the house was all fixed.

"Now the house looks very nice!" said Lion.

"Let's get back to where we sit," said Frog.

TAKE-HOME BOOK
BLUE WATERS
Use with "Punky Goes Fishing."

Who Are We?
by Tanner Ottley Gay

HARCOURT BRACE & COMPANY

Harcourt Brace & Company material copyrighted under notice appearing earlier in this work.

Who am I? Would you like my job? Whose job would you like best?

12

Our job is to keep you safe. Next to your mom and dad, we're the ones who look out for you. Do you know who we are?

1

What do we do?

2

I have pigs, cows, and horses.
I am very kind to them. I keep pigs, cows, and horses together in one place. Do you know who I am?

11

Who are we?

10

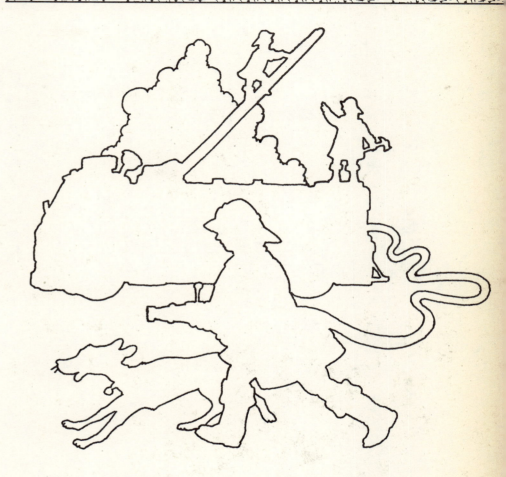

Who knows when you may need us? You will not have to wait. We'll be there in our big, red truck. Do you know who we are?

3

Who are we?

We love to run and jump about. Our job is to make you happy. I bet you've wanted to be like us. Do you know who we are?

Who am I?

8

You may see me the next time you're swimming. I'm the one who goes into the water to keep you safe. Do you know who I am?

5

Who am I?

I've just checked a boy's teeth. They look very good. I want all of you to have good teeth. Do you know who I am?

TAKE-HOME BOOK
BLUE WATERS
Use with "Father Bear Comes Home."

by Marie Richards

HARCOURT BRACE & COMPANY

Harcourt Brace & Company material copyrighted under notice appearing earlier in this work.

Tommy was a baby frog. He couldn't wait to be big. One day he asked his mother what he would be when he was big.

"Mother, will I be a whale?" asked Tommy.

"Yes," laughed Tommy. "I know how to jump out of the water now. I'm not too little. I'm a real frog at last!"

"No," laughed Mother. "You will not be a whale!"

"Then will I be a real boat with a big sail?" asked Tommy.

"No, Tommy!" laughed Mother. "You will not be a boat with a sail!"

"That was a nice boy," said Tommy. "He let us go!"

"And you are a nice frog," said Mother. "You said that you were too little to come out of the water. But you were not too little to come and look for me."

"The river is the best place for you," said the boy. "You don't belong to me. I know you will be happy here."

Out jumped Tommy and his mother. They jumped along the river. At last they were happy.

"Then what will I be?" asked Tommy.

"Someday you will be a frog like me, Tommy," said Mother.

"Will I have real legs someday, too?" asked Tommy.

"Yes, you will," laughed Mother.

Soon Tommy did get real legs.

"Look, Mom, I have legs!" said Tommy.

"So you do," said Mother. "Now you can get out of the water."

"No, I can't," said Tommy. "I don't know how. I'm too little."

"You are not too little, Tommy. You can get out of the water," Mother said.

The boy put the lid on the box. Then he walked very fast.

"Where are we going?" asked Tommy.

"I don't know," said Mother.

Soon the boy stopped and took the lid off the box.

"Oh!" said the boy. "Now I have a big frog and a little frog! Is this your mother, little frog? Did you miss her?"

Just then, a boy came along. He picked up Tommy's mother and put her in a box!

"A real frog!" said the boy. "I will take it with me!"

"Oh, no!" said Tommy. "I need to stop him. I need to get out of the water."

"Mother said that I can get out of the water. She said that I am not too little. I will try."

With that, Tommy jumped out of the water. He hopped very fast along the river. At last he saw the boy.

Tommy jumped into the box with his mother.

"Tommy!" said Mother. "You did get out of the water! You are a good frog. Now we need to get out of this box."

TAKE-HOME BOOK
BLUE WATERS
Use with "The Cake That Mack Ate."

HARCOURT BRACE & COMPANY

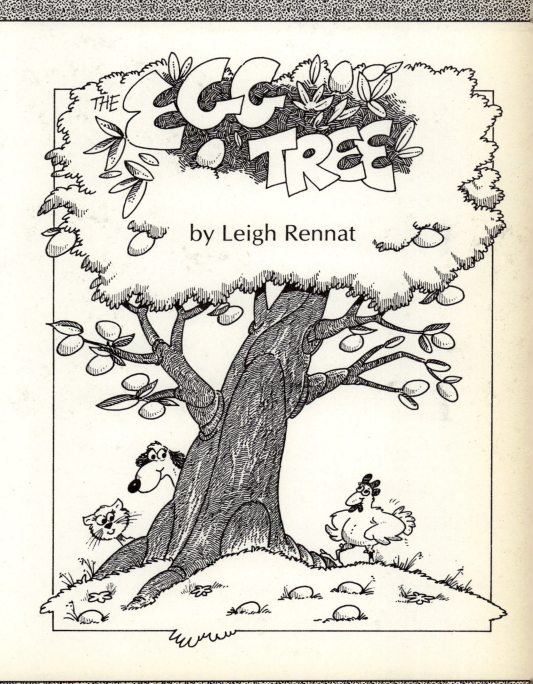

THE EGG TREE

by Leigh Rennat

Harcourt Brace & Company material copyrighted under notice appearing earlier in this work.

Every day Mrs. Posy gets eggs from her tree. And every day she says, "Thank you, Helen!"

Could eggs grow on a tree? What do you think?

Mrs. Posy was a very happy woman. She had a cat, a dog, four fish, and a nice hen named Helen.

Every day Helen laid one egg. Every day Mrs. Posy said, "Thank you, Helen!"

Mrs. Posy would keep the eggs to make a cake. She made very good cakes.

"These look like eggs," said one friend.

"They ARE eggs," said Mrs. Posy. "These eggs are just like Helen's."

Mrs. Posy gave Helen a big hug.

"My friends," she said. "Take all the eggs you want. This is an egg tree!"

Then one morning Mrs. Posy's friends yelled, "Get up! Get up! Come and see your tree!"

Mrs. Posy made cakes for her friends. They were so good that her friends ate her cakes up fast.

One day a friend said, "We love your cakes. Why don't you make and sell these cakes?"

Mrs. Posy laughed. "That would be nice," she said, "but I would need a lot more eggs. My hen, Helen, gives me one egg each day."

"Wouldn't it be nice if eggs grew on trees?" laughed her friend.

"Yes, it would," said Mrs. Posy.

Soon a tree came up.
The tree grew and grew . . . and grew!

Now Helen was trying to dig a hole. Mrs. Posy laughed.

"See, Helen," she said. "I will plant your egg."

So Mrs. Posy planted the egg. She watered it every day.

That night, Mrs. Posy had a dream about her hen.

In the dream, Helen said, "Take my next egg and plant it. Soon you will have all the eggs you need."

The next morning Mrs. Posy said, "What a silly dream that was!" Then she went out to get an egg from Helen.

"Thank you, Helen," she said as she took the egg.

Helen jumped down and flapped and flapped.

"What a silly hen!" laughed Mrs. Posy. "What are you trying to say?"

Then Mrs. Posy took a look at the egg. It did not look like the other eggs.

"I know the dream I had was silly," she said. "But I don't know why this egg looks so silly."

TAKE-HOME BOOK
BLUE WATERS
Use with "Lionel at Large."

My Friend, Judy

by Patricia Ann Becker

HARCOURT BRACE & COMPANY

Harcourt Brace & Company material copyrighted under notice appearing earlier in this work.

Judy is my best friend. I think I am her best friend, too.

Hi! My name is Happy. I am a dog. Do you see that girl over there? Her name is Judy. She is my friend.

I think Judy is very nice. She always brings my food to me before she eats.

I think I will keep Judy. She is a good friend. She does just what I say. I do just what she says. We always like each other.

Judy had mud all over her. I was glad that she took a bath. I was not glad when I had to get a bath. I just hate baths! Don't you?

When I want Judy to try some of my food, she doesn't want it. Judy thinks that dog food is just for dogs.

Judy and I always like to play together. One day Judy was looking for me. I think she was having fun looking for me.

"Don't run away from me any more!" she said.

I think she was a bit mad. Judy doesn't get mad at me very much.

I watched her look all over. At last she looked by the shelf. Judy still didn't see me. I began biting the rug and pulling on it.

I was having so much fun running. Then I ran into the mud. Judy ran into the mud, too. She didn't like the mud very much.

Then Judy looked down and saw me.

"Don't hide from me any more!" she laughed.

I got a big hug from her. I think she missed me.

One day I took Judy out for a walk. We were having fun on our walk. I think she liked it when I ran away from her.

TAKE-HOME BOOK
BLUE WATERS
Use with "Frog and Toad Together."

The Flying Turtle

by Tanner Ottley Gay

HARCOURT BRACE & COMPANY

Harcourt Brace & Company material copyrighted under notice appearing earlier in this work.

Turtle was at the beach. He climbed up to the top of a rock and jumped off. Down he went. Plop! "Oh, no!" yelled Turtle.

After that day Turtle always says, "Take it from me. What you can do is better than something you can't do!"

Eagle was flying around the beach. She flew over to see Turtle.

"Is there something I can do, Turtle?" she asked.

"No, I was just trying to fly," said Turtle. "I wish I could fly like you, Eagle."

Eagle flew down to the water as fast as she could.

"Are you OK, Turtle?" she asked.

"Yes, Eagle," said Turtle. "But my flying days are over!"

"Turtle! Oh, no!" said Eagle.
Down, down went Turtle into the water.
PLOP!

Eagle laughed. "Some days I wish I had a house on my back like you, Turtle! But only turtles can ever have houses on their backs, and only birds can fly. That's just the way it is."

Up, up they flew.

"I'm flying! I'm flying!" Turtle yelled out.

Many of Turtle's friends were down on the beach.

"Look at Turtle!" they said.

When Turtle saw his friends, he just didn't think. He did not hold on the way he should have.

"Hello, down there!" he yelled.

"I know I'm not a bird, but I want to fly like a bird," said Turtle. "There has to be some way. Can you take me flying, Eagle?"

"I don't know if I should do that, Turtle," said Eagle. "It's not safe for you. You're better off here on the beach."

But Turtle did not stop trying. He asked Eagle many times to take him flying. Eagle always said no.

At last one day, Eagle said, "Turtle, I don't think I should do it, but I will take you flying."

Turtle climbed up on Eagle's back. "Now, you have to hold on," said Eagle. "Don't let go!"

TAKE-HOME BOOK
BLUE WATERS
Use with "The Doorbell Rang."

HARCOURT BRACE & COMPANY

Baby Day
by William Lakin

Harcourt Brace & Company material copyrighted under notice appearing earlier in this work.

Then we all took the baby to see the ten little pigs, the three pups, the two kittens, and the calf!

12

Mr. and Mrs. Lopez have the house next door to ours. They are always very nice to us. We just love to go over there.

11

This morning Mrs. Lopez asked us to come over. She said she had something for us to see.

"What could it be?" we asked each other.

We all sat down and ate some cake. Then Tina, one of Mr. and Mrs. Lopez's children, came in.

"Oh, look at the baby!" we all said.

"That's not all," said Mr. Lopez. "Come in the house and have some cake. They should be here soon."

"Who?" we asked.

Mr. and Mrs. Lopez just laughed.

We all ran to the Lopez's front door. We rang and rang, but nobody was there.

"Perhaps they are not home," I said.

Then we saw a note by the door.

Dear Children,
  Come out back.
It's Baby Day!

Love,
  Mr. and Mrs. Lopez

We all ran to the pig pen. A mother pig had ten little pigs.
I laughed and said, "Now I know why you said this is Baby Day."

"Oh, look at the three pups!" we all said.

"That's not all," said Mrs. Lopez. "Come and see the pigs."

We ran out back and said hello.

"Why did you say this is Baby Day?" I asked.

"Come and see for yourselves," said Mr. Lopez.

"Oh, look!" we all said. "The cow has a little calf!"

"That's not all," said Mrs. Lopez. "Come over here."

"Look at the two kittens!" Tommy said.

"That's not all," said Mr. Lopez. "Come this way."

TAKE-HOME BOOK
HOLD ON TIGHT
Use with "Peace at Last."

HARCOURT BRACE & COMPANY

GO TO SLEEP!

by Tanner Ottley Gay

© Harcourt Brace & Company material copyrighted under notice appearing earlier in this work.

All the birds were tired and wanted to go to sleep. All, that is, but Little Bird. He was just getting started!

"Tweet, tweet! Tweet, tweet!" said Little Bird, running around the room.

Soon, Grandma Bird stopped tweeting. "Little Bird," she said, "now you can tweet and I'll hum."
But Little Bird was fast asleep.

"My Little Bird is asleep at last," laughed Grandma Bird. "We will have to play Keep Awake every night!"

"It's time to sleep now, Little Bird," said Mother Bird. "We need a little peace around here!"

"But I'm not tired," said Little Bird.

"You're never tired!" laughed Father Bird.

Little Bird started humming, and Grandma Bird started tweeting. She tweeted,

"Keep awake, keep awake,
keep awake till morning light.
Keep awake, keep awake,
we'll be wide awake all night . . ."

Grandma Bird tweeted and tweeted. Little Bird hummed and hummed.

"You must sit with me and hum to yourself as I tweet to you. Then, when I stop tweeting, you will tweet while I hum."

Little Bird couldn't believe Grandma Bird was going to play with him. "Let's get started," he said.

"Look at the clock, Little Bird," said Grandpa Bird. "It's time for all of us to go to sleep."

"But I'm wide awake," said Little Bird. "Can't I play a little more?"

"All right," said Father Bird. "But just a little bit."

Little Bird played by himself. He started to tweet. Then he started hopping around. Soon all the birds were awake.

"All right, Little Bird," said Mother Bird. "No more playing for you. You are going to sleep right now!"

Grandma Bird said, "To play Keep Awake, we both have to be up all night. No sleeping at all!"

"This will be fun," said Little Bird. "How do you play?"

Grandma Bird went over to Little Bird. "You and I can play," she said. "We'll play Keep Awake."

"Keep Awake? I've never played that," said Little Bird.

"I will try my best," said Little Bird. He sat very still. His legs wanted to hop. His beak wanted to tweet.

"No hopping, legs!" yelled Little Bird. "No tweeting, beak!"

Little Bird sat still. His legs still wanted to hop. His beak still wanted to tweet.

"I said no hopping, legs! No tweeting, beak. Now, do what I tell you!" Little Bird yelled.

Now all the Birds were awake. "Little Bird, what are you doing?" asked Father Bird.

"My legs and beak will not do what I say," said Little Bird. "They just want to play."

"What are we going to do with you?" asked Father Bird.

Then Grandma Bird said, "I think I know what to do."

TAKE-HOME BOOK
HOLD ON TIGHT
Use with "Dreams."

Marco's Day

by Patricia Ann Becker

HARCOURT BRACE & COMPANY

© Harcourt Brace & Company material copyrighted under notice appearing earlier in this work.

Next, a shell tree walked in and gave us each a shell.
"Now I believe you," said my mom.
"Me, too!" said my dad.
"At last!" I laughed. "What a silly day this has been!"

What a day this has been! I just can't believe all I have seen! Let me tell you about my day.

It all started this morning while Dad was reading the paper.
"Good morning," said the paper.
"Who said that?" asked Dad.
"Not me," I said.
"I thought someone said something," said Dad.

Then a bug with a hat on climbed up Dad's sleeve.
"That bug has a hat on!" yelled Dad.
"Yes, I know," I said.

Just then the paper began to talk.
"Hello, Marco! How are you?" it said.
"I'm fine," I said while smiling at Mom and Dad.

10

"Good morning," said the paper.
"Dad, the paper talked!"
"No," laughed Dad. "That was you talking."
"No, Dad, I didn't talk," I said. "It was the paper!"

3

Then I saw something silly while I was at school. We have a paper city in our room. There are streets and houses in the city. I was standing by the city when I saw it. It was a bug with a hat on! The bug was walking across one of the city streets.

4

"Oh," said my mom.
"That's nice," said my dad.
"Then I saw a shell tree on my way home."
Mom and Dad just smiled.

9

While we were eating, I began telling Mom and Dad about my day.
"The paper said good morning to Dad," I began. "Then, at school, I saw a bug with a hat on."

"Look!" I yelled. "There's a bug in the city! It has a hat on."
The others started turning around to see it, too.
"Where is the bug with the hat on?" they asked. "We don't see it."
"It was there. I saw it!" I said. They just laughed.

I saw something silly while walking home from school, too. I couldn't believe it. There in front of me was a shell tree. I picked some shells to bring home.
"Now they will believe me," I thought.
I let my mom see the shells.

"Where did you get these?" she asked.
"I picked them off a shell tree," I said.
"Oh, Marco," laughed Mom. "You are silly!"
"But I DID pick them off a shell tree," I said.
Mom just laughed.

TAKE-HOME BOOK
HOLD ON TIGHT
Use with "Stars."

SUNNY AND FUNNY BUNNY

by Carol Peske

HARCOURT BRACE & COMPANY

© Harcourt Brace & Company material copyrighted under notice appearing earlier in this work.

Sunny and Funny Bunny had been inside all day long.

"Mother, may Funny and I go out and play?" asked Sunny.

"You may go out after we eat," said Mother.

"I've had enough of hide-and-seek," said Sunny. "Let's just look at the stars."

"We could look at them for a long, long time," said Funny.

"Yes," laughed Sunny. "Then you cannot play a trick on me for a long, long time!"

Sunny and Funny ate all their food.
"I've had enough food," said Funny.
"Me, too!" said Sunny. "May we go out now?"

"You ARE a funny bunny," said Sunny.
"Let's play some more," said Funny. "Do you want to play hide-and-seek or some other game?"

"Whose coat and hat are these?" asked Sunny.

"They belong to my friend," said Funny. "I used them just to trick you. Why do you think my name is Funny?"

"Yes, you may, but don't go far," said Mother. "It will soon be time for bed."

"We will be close by," said Sunny and Funny.

When they got outside, they saw a bright star.

"That star glows like the sun," said Sunny.

"Yes, it's as bright as a star can be," said Funny.

"Funny, where are you?" yelled Sunny. "This is not FUNNY! Come out now!"

"Here I am!" said Funny.

Then Sunny saw a blue hat by a log.

"I see you," said Sunny.

She ran over to the log and picked up the blue hat. Funny was not with the hat.

"Let's play hide-and-seek," said Funny.

"You hide," said Sunny. "I'll seek. One, two, three, four, five, six," said Sunny. "Here I come!"

Sunny looked around for Funny and could not see him.

"Funny, where are you?" asked Sunny.

Then Sunny saw a blue coat sticking out of a little tree.

"I see you," said Sunny.

She ran to the tree and pulled on the coat. Funny was not in the coat.

TAKE-HOME BOOK
HOLD ON TIGHT
Use with "There's an Alligator Under My Bed."

HARCOURT BRACE & COMPANY

Where's the Kitten?

by Richard Christopher

Harcourt Brace & Company material copyrighted under notice appearing earlier in this work.

"Why did you two kittens climb up the trees?" asked the woman.
The kittens looked at the woman. Then they looked at Meg. Then they looked at each other.

"They will never tell us," Meg laughed, "but we have them back now. Thank you for Muffin!" said Meg.
"Thank you for Peaches!" said the woman.

Meg couldn't find Muffin, her kitten, anywhere. Meg had looked everywhere. She had even looked in the car and in the garage. There was no Muffin.

Now it was night, and it was getting cold. Meg sat on the stairs and thought about Muffin. She didn't want to leave Muffin outside at night.

"It's time to come in now," said Meg's mom.

Mom and Meg took the kitten to the woman's house. The woman came to the door, holding a kitten.

"Muffin!" said Meg.
"Peaches!" said the woman.
"Muffin, I'm so glad to see you," said Meg.
Muffin looked happy.
Peaches looked happy to see the woman, too.

Mom talked to the woman who had put the ad in the paper. The woman's house was on the same street as Meg's house.
"What did she say?" Meg asked.
"I can't believe it. I think that she has our kitten and we have hers," said Mom.
"She said we could come right over."

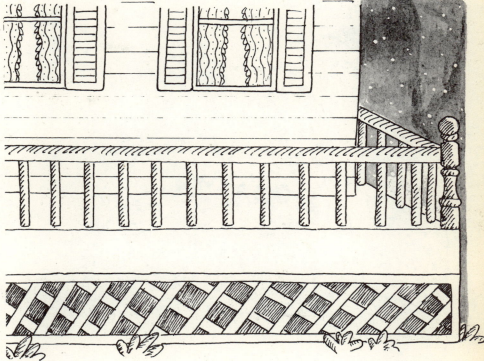

"Please, Mom," said Meg. "Just let me look a little more."
"All right," said Mom. "I'll come out and help you."
Mom and Meg looked for Muffin together.

After a while, Meg thought she saw something up in a tree.
"Look!" said Meg. "I think Muffin is up in that tree."
Mom thought she saw the kitten, too.
"We have to get him down."
"I'll go up the tree," said Meg.

Two days passed. Muffin was still missing. Mom and Meg were looking at their ad in the paper.

Then Mom saw an ad about two other kittens. It was just like Mom and Meg's ad. It said one kitten was still lost and the other kitten had jumped up in a tree.

"Yes," said Meg, petting the kitten. "What are we going to do with this kitten?"

"Why don't we put an ad in the paper?" said Mom. "In the ad, we can tell about this kitten. We can ask if anyone has seen Muffin, too."

"I'll help you with the ad," said Meg.

"No," said Mom. "You wait down here. I'll go up."

"OK, Mom, but be careful."

"I'll be careful," said Mom as she went up.

"Oh, no!" said Mom.

"Is Muffin all right?" asked Meg.

"Well," said Mom. "This kitten is all right, but it's not Muffin."

Mom picked up the kitten and came back down.

"You're right," said Meg. "That's not Muffin." She looked as if she were going to cry.

"We'll find your kitten, Meg," said Mom. "Would you like to pet this one?"

TAKE-HOME BOOK
HOLD ON TIGHT
Use with "Henry and Mudge in Puddle Trouble."

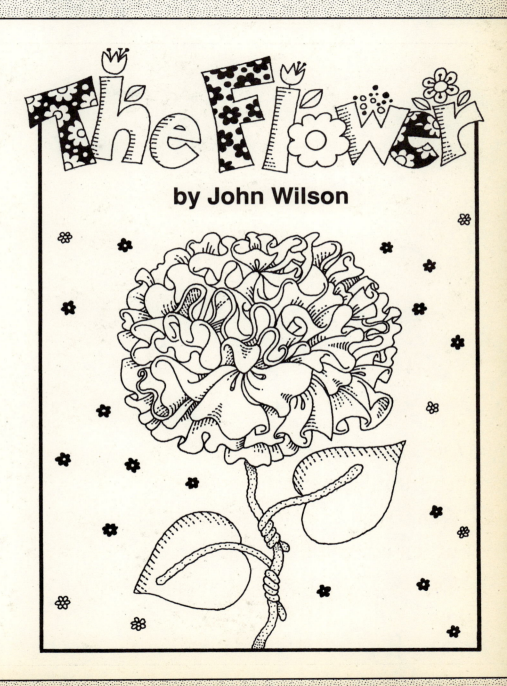

The Flower
by John Wilson

HARCOURT BRACE & COMPANY

Harcourt Brace & Company material copyrighted under notice appearing earlier in this work.

We all saw how to make paper flowers. Soon there were flowers all over. But no one made a flower as pretty as Kim's.

Snow is very pretty, and it's fun to play in. But I was getting tired of snow. My friends at school were getting tired of snow, too.

One day, while we were at school, more snow started to come down.

"Oh, no!" said Tasha, holding her head.

"I can't stand it," Jamal said. "Enough is enough!"

Everyone laughed because we all knew what they were talking about.

Mr. Lund smiled. "The snow will be over very soon," he said.

"Yes, I do," said Kim. "I made a paper flower and stuck it in my cup. I knew my flower would not grow before the flower day."

"Good thinking, Kim!" laughed Mr. Lund. "Why don't you tell us how you made your flower? Then we can make some more for Flower Day."

"It's because it's in a paper cup," she laughed. "Didn't you know that paper cups grow into paper flowers?"

Then Kim started laughing. We all started laughing together.

"Do you have something to tell us, Kim?" asked Mr. Lund.

"I think we need something bright and pretty right now. What do you think?"

"Why don't we plan a Flower Day?" I said. "We could plant flowers in our room."

"Yes!" said Tasha. "Then we could ask other children to come see our flowers."

Everyone thought it would be fun to have a Flower Day.

The next day we each planted our own flower. We knew the flowers would take a while to grow. We watered them every day. Jamal talked to his flower.

4

"Kim's flower is not like the others," I thought. Then I touched it.

"Kim," I said. "Your flower is made of paper. How did you grow a paper flower?"

We all looked at Kim. She just smiled.

9

Every day we did nice things for our flowers. At last the flowers started growing. Jamal's flower was growing fast. My flower started growing a little. But Kim's flower was not growing at all.

One morning I came to school and saw the children around Kim's flower.

"Did it grow?" I asked.

"Yes," Jamal said. "Look! It's the best flower here!"

"It came up later than all the others, but I knew it would grow," smiled Kim.

"Why isn't my flower growing?" asked Kim.

"It will grow. Let's just wait and see," said Mr. Lund.

Kim waited and waited. All the other plants grew a little bit each day. Kim's flower still did not grow.

Soon the Flower Day was near. Kim was thinking about planting a new flower because hers still was not growing. She knew her flower would not grow in time for Flower Day.

TAKE-HOME BOOK
HOLD ON TIGHT
Use with "All About Seeds."

HARCOURT BRACE & COMPANY

by Carol Peske

Harcourt Brace & Company material copyrighted under notice appearing earlier in this work.

"Toot the Tugboat is saved! We love you, Toot the Tugboat!" yelled the people.

"Toot the Tugboat loves you, too," said Toot.

Toot the Tugboat had been pulling big ships up the river for a long, long time. All the ships knew Toot, and Toot knew all the ships.

Toot met the ships as they came into the river from the sea. He pulled the ships up the river to the docks. People loved to see Toot pulling ships. They smiled and waved to him as he went by.

"Yes," said a woman. "I think people would come to see a real tugboat."

"I like it!" said the man who ran Toot. "Toot could stay here, and people could come to see him."

That same day, a man was out planting seeds near the docks. Seeing the line of people made him think of a way to save Toot.

"Look how many people are lining up to see Toot one last time. Don't you think people would line up to see him every day?" asked the man.

One day, Toot was pulling a ship up the river in the rain. The ship was loaded with fruit and other foods for the people and the animals of the city. Toot was very tired and wet, and he was going very slowly. He didn't think he was going to make it to the docks.

Then Toot just stopped and couldn't start.

"What's the matter?" asked the ship Toot was pulling.

"I can't go on," said Toot. "I'm just too tired."

Toot the Tugboat was going to be pulled out of the water the next day. Toot was sad, but he also knew that he couldn't pull ships anymore. Many people came to see Toot one last time.

People came to the docks and shouted, "Save Toot the Tugboat! Save Toot the Tugboat!"

But Toot could not be fixed. He was just too old.

Soon a boat pulled up to help. Some people came to see if they could get Toot started. But they couldn't make him go.

They had to get a new tugboat to pull Toot to the docks. Toot was too tired to say no. He just let the new tugboat pull him along. It felt good to rest.

There was a lot of talk about Toot on the docks. Some people thought Toot's days as a tugboat were over. Other people thought Toot should be fixed.

TAKE-HOME BOOK
HOLD ON TIGHT
Use with "Henny Penny."

HARCOURT BRACE & COMPANY

by Mary Clark

Harcourt Brace & Company material copyrighted under notice appearing earlier in this work.

Hap and the camels set off on their trip. For the camels this trip is like any other trip. For Hap, the trip is something she has only dreamed of.

12

Hap is a very happy horse. She has many friends. Cam and Bumpy are her very best friends.

1

Hap, Cam, and Bumpy do everything together. They play games together. They eat dinner together. They take walks together. But there is one thing the three friends cannot do together.

"I wish you could come, too, Raj," says Hap.

"I have to stay here and look after things," says Raj. "I'll be here when you get back."

"Thank you, Raj," says Hap. "You have made me such a happy horse."

The next morning the sun is out and the sky is blue. Raj puts the packs on Hap's back and fills them with water.

"When you need water, just let someone know, Hap," says Raj. "There is enough water here to last the trip."

Cam and Bumpy get to go on long trips. Hap has to stay at home. This morning all the camels are going on a trip.

"They'll be back," says Raj, the man who feeds Hap. "You stay here with me."

"Why can't I go with them?" asks Hap.

"They are going on a long trip," says Raj. "There is no water along the way. Camels don't need much water. You are a horse, Hap."

"Let's try them on you," says Raj as he puts the packs on Hap's back.

"It's like having a hump on each side," says Hap. "Thank you, Raj."

"Those look great on you!" say Cam and Bumpy. "We are going on a long trip in the morning. Now you can go with us!"

Hap can't wait until morning.

Raj brings out two packs. Hap can't believe his eyes. These packs don't look like the packs on the camels. These packs were made just for him. They will hold lots of water. Now he can go on long trips with the camels.

"Do I need more water than a camel?" asks Hap.

"Yes, you do," says Raj.

Raj sees that Hap looks sad.

"Will they be gone long?" asks Hap.

"Yes, they will, Hap," says Raj. "But they always come back."

At last the camels are back. Cam and Bumpy tell a story about the great time they had. Hap wishes she had gone with them. Raj wishes he could think of a way for Hap to go next time.

6

One day after dinner, Raj says that he has a surprise for Hap. Hap can't wait to see what it is.

7

TAKE-HOME BOOK
HOLD ON TIGHT
Use with "Lost!"

HARCOURT BRACE & COMPANY

A Day at the Park

by Patricia Ann Becker

Harcourt Brace & Company material copyrighted under notice appearing earlier in this work.

There was no school today. I wanted to do something fun. I called my friend Taro to come over. He always has good ideas about what to do.

At the end of the day, Taro said, "Let's do this again sometime!"

"Yes," I said. "But next time let's not bring so much stuff!"

Taro and I both laughed.

"Let's go to the park for the day," he said.

"That's a great idea!" I said. "Let's go!"

"Wait," said Taro. "We will need to take some things."

So that's just what we did. First, we ate all the picnic food. Then we looked at our books. We made some pictures. Then the cat scared away a make-believe mouse. No one got hurt, so we took turns resting on the cot. Our day at the park turned out to be a lot of fun.

"Do you have any more ideas?" I asked Taro.

"No," he said. "Do you?"

"Yes," I said. "Let's make believe we are at the park! We have all the stuff we need."

"That's a great idea," said Taro.

"What do you want to take?" I asked.

"Let's take a picnic lunch," said Taro.

"Great idea! I'll pack it," I said.

"Now we can go," said Taro.

"Wait," I said. "We should take some books."

"Great idea!" said Taro. "I'll get some."

"Now, let's go," I said.

"I'll get the picnic lunch and the books," I said.

"I'll get the pens and paper and the cat ," said Taro.

We both ran fast to get all the stuff. Boy, did we get wet!

"Now we can go to the park," said Taro.

"No, wait," I said. "Do you hear what I hear?"

"I don't know," said Taro. "What do you hear?"

"I think I hear rain," I said.

"I don't believe it!" yelled Taro. "It's raining! Let's bring all the stuff in!"

"Wait! We need some pens and paper," Taro said, pointing to the desk.

"Why do we need pens and paper?" I asked.

"So we can make pictures at the park," said Taro.

"Great idea!" I said. "I'll get them."

"We can go now," said Taro.

"No, wait," I said.

"Again?" asked Taro.

"One more time," I laughed. "We should take the cat with us."

"Why take the cat?" asked Taro.

"If we see a mouse, the cat can scare it away," I said.

"Great!" said Taro. "I'll get the cat."

"Let's go!" I said.

"Wait," said Taro.

"What now?" I asked.

"We need to bring a cot," said Taro.

"We won't need a cot!" I told Taro.

"Yes, we will," he said. "If we get hurt, we may need to lie down."

"Oh," I said. "I'll get the cot."

TAKE-HOME BOOK
HOLD ON TIGHT
Use with "Jamaica's Find."

HARCOURT BRACE & COMPANY

by Marie Richards

Harcourt Brace & Company material copyrighted under notice appearing earlier in this work.

Dad and Carmen tasted it.

"It doesn't taste very good," said Dad.

"But it does taste big," laughed Carmen.

"It's a big cake with a big taste," said Kate with a smile.

"Next time, let's just make a little cake that tastes good," laughed Carmen.

It was very gray day. Soon it began to rain. Carmen was playing alone inside. "This is not much fun," she thought. "I'm going to think of something else to do."

"Dad, would you like to do something?"

"Sure," said Dad. "What do you want to do?"

Carmen thought for a while. Then she had an idea.

"Let's taste it," said Kate. "It still might be good." Kate took a little bite.

"Is it any good?" Carmen asked.

"What do you think?" asked Dad.

"Taste it yourselves," said Kate.

"Did you put some of this in the cake mix?" asked Dad, pointing to a little can.

"Yes. You said to add some," said Carmen.

"How much did you add?" asked Dad.

"Just a cup," said Carmen.

"Oh, I see," smiled Dad. "I think I have found out why the cake is so big. This makes the cake rise."

"Do you think we put in too much?" asked Carmen.

"I know you put in too much!" laughed Dad.

"Dad, would you help me bake a cake?" asked Carmen.

"Sure," said Dad. "Let's get started! First we must get everything we need. You get out a few eggs and the pans. I'll get out the other things."

"What should I do with the eggs?" Carmen asked.

"Lay them down over there. But don't drop them!" laughed Dad.

Just then the doorbell rang. It was Kate, Carmen's friend from next door.

"What are you doing?" Kate asked.

"Dad and I are baking a cake," said Carmen. "Do you want to help?"

"Sure!" said Kate.

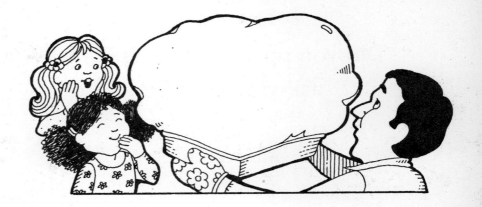

They were all surprised when they saw the size of the cake.

"What a big cake!" said Dad. "I can't believe it!"

Kate and Carmen couldn't stop laughing.

"That cake is almost as big as me," laughed Kate.

"Are you sure there are no cows hiding under that cake?" asked Carmen.

Kate and Carmen stood around waiting while the cake was baking. It seemed to take a long time.

"Is it almost done?" Carmen asked her dad.

"Almost," said Dad.

"It sure smells good," said Kate.

At last the bell rang. Dad came and took out the cake.

Carmen and Kate started mixing the cake together.

"Now, all we need to add is some of this," said Dad.

Just then the doorbell rang. Carmen's dad went to the door.

"Dad said all we need to add is some of this," said Carmen. "Do you think one cup will be enough?"

"Yes, that looks about right," Kate said.

"Let's see," said Dad when he came back from the door. "Where were we?"

"We put everything in, Dad," said Carmen. "Now it's time to bake it."

"Great!" said Dad. "Let's bake it!"